DANIIL KARABUT

90s Fashion Trends

How to Replicate the Decade's Best Looks

"I think that '90s fashion was about comfort and individuality. It was about rejecting traditional beauty standards and celebrating diversity and inclusivity."

Winona Ryder

Contents

Foreword

The 90s was a decade of iconic fashion trends that inspire modern style today. From grunge-inspired looks to minimalist beauty routines, the 90s was a time of creativity and individuality that produced some of the most memorable fashion moments ever.

This book will explore the most critical 90s fashion trends and how to replicate them in a modern context. From the grunge trend to hip-hop fashion, we'll examine how these trends were born and how they continue to inspire stylish style today.

But this book isn't just about replicating 90s fashion trends - it's also about celebrating this decade's creativity, individuality, and self-expression. The 90s was a time of rejecting traditional glamour and embracing a more casual and rugged aesthetic. It was a time of fusing different styles and cultures to create something new and unique.

As we explore the world of 90s fashion, we'll also examine the significance of these trends and their impact on the fashion industry. By rediscovering these trends and embracing their spirit of creativity and individuality, we can create a fashion landscape that celebrates diversity, inclusivity, and self-expression.

So join us on this journey through the world of 90s fashion, and discover how this decade continues to inspire modern style today.

Preface

As a lover of fashion and style, I've always been fascinated by the unique and creative trends that emerged in the 90s. From grunge-inspired looks to minimalist beauty routines, the 90s was a time of experimentation and individuality that produced some of the most iconic fashion moments ever.

But as someone who grew up in the 2000s, I often found replicating these trends in a modern context difficult. I wanted to incorporate the spirit of 90s fashion into my style, but I wasn't sure how to do so without looking like I was stuck in a time capsule.

I decided to write this book - to explore the most critical 90s fashion trends and how to replicate them in a modern context. Through research and experimentation, I've discovered how to incorporate the creativity, individuality, and self-expression of 90s fashion into my style, and I want to share that knowledge with you.

This book will explore the most critical 90s fashion trends and how to replicate them in a modern context. From grunge to hip hop, from minimalist beauty routines to the iconic looks of the red carpet, we'll examine how these trends were born and how they continue to inspire modern fashion today.

But this book isn't just about replicating 90s fashion trends - it's also about celebrating the spirit of creativity and indi- viduality that characterized this decade. By embracing the unique movements and styles of the 90s, we can create a fashion landscape that celebrates diversity, inclusivity, and self-expression.

I hope this book inspires you to embrace the creativity and individuality of 90s fashion and incorporate these trends into your style. Let's rediscover the iconic fashion moments of the 90s and celebrate the enduring legacy of this decade on modern style.

Acknowledgement

I want to express my gratitude to all those who contributed to the creation of this book. This project would not have been possible without their support, guidance, and encouragement.

First and foremost, I would like to thank my family and friends for their unwavering support throughout the writing process. Your encouragement, feedback, and enthusiasm kept me motivated and inspired.

I would also like to thank my editor and the publishing team for their guidance and expertise. Your insights and suggestions helped shape this book into its final form.

I am grateful to the fashion designers, stylists, models, and photographers who created the iconic fashion moments of the 90s. Your creativity and individuality continue to inspire modern fashion today.

Finally, I would like to thank the readers of this book for their interest in 90s fashion trends. I hope this book inspires you to embrace the spirit of creativity and individuality that characterized this decade and incorporate these trends into your style.

Thank you all for your contributions to this project.

Introduction: Setting the Stage for 90s Fashion Trends

The 1990s was a decade of bold and memorable fashion trends influencing modern style. From grunge and minimalism to hip-hop and retro, the 90s was a time of experimentation and creativity that produced some of the most iconic looks in fashion history. Whether you lived through the decade or discovered it for the first time, there's no denying the lasting impact of 90s fashion trends.

In this book, we'll explore the most influential fashion trends of the 90s and show you how to replicate them for today's fashion scene. We'll deeply dive into grunge, minimalism, hip-hop, retro, street style, and other fashion movements that defined the decade. You'll learn to incorporate these trends into your wardrobe and accessorize them with a modern twist.

Through this book, you'll discover how 90s fashion continues to inspire designers and fashion lovers today. Whether you're a fashionista looking to add a touch of nostalgia to your style or simply interested in the history of fashion, this book is for you. So, let's travel back in time to the decade of flannel shirts, high-waisted jeans, and platform shoes and explore the best fashion trends of the 90s.

Grunge - How to Replicate the Ultimate Anti-Fashion Look

In the early 1990s, a new fashion trend emerged, characterized by its anti-fashion aesthetic. Grunge fashion was born out of punk and alternative music scenes and was about rejecting mainstream fashion norms. Grunge fashion was defined by oversized, casual, and grubby-looking clothing, often layered and accessorized with leather, plaid, and chains. Grunge's style directly contrasted with the elegant and glamorous fashion of the 80s, focusing on individuality, authenticity, and rebellion.

To replicate the ultimate grunge look, start with an oversized flannel shirt, a band t-shirt, or a plain white t-shirt. Pair this with ripped or faded jeans or distressed denim shorts. Grunge fashion is all about layering, so add an oversized sweater or cardigan over your shirt and wear a denim jacket or a leather jacket for extra warmth. For shoes, opt for a pair of combat boots, Dr. Martens, or sneakers with a worn-out look.

Accessories are an essential part of grunge fashion. Wear a beanie or a beret on your head, and add some chains or studded jewelry to your outfit. Grunge fashion is about simplicity and comfort, so keep your makeup minimal and natural. Go for a matte finish with a dark lipstick shade, and add some smudged eyeliner for a touch of edge.

Incorporating grunge fashion into your wardrobe is a great way to add a touch of rebellion and authenticity to your style. Whether you're going for a whole grunge look, or just incorporating a few elements into your outfit, the key is to embrace the nonconformist spirit of the 90s and have fun with your fashion choices.

Minimalism - How to Achieve Chic Simplicity

Minimalism was a defining trend of the 90s that emphasized clean lines, simple shapes, and neutral colors. Minimalist fashion was a reaction to the excesses of the 80s and a return to simplicity and elegance. Minimalism was all about quality over quantity, focusing on essential pieces that could be mixed and matched to create various looks.

Pair a basic white or black t-shirt with tailored trousers or a midi-length skirt to achieve a chic minimalist look. Opt for simple and classic pieces that are well-made and timeless. Avoid loud prints and patterns; focus on solid colors and subtle textures.

Accessories are essential in minimalist fashion but should be simple and understated. Opt for a delicate necklace or stud earrings, and keep your handbag simple and unadorned. For shoes, choose a pair of classic loafers or simple heels.

Makeup and hair should be natural and effortless, focusing on healthy skin and simple hairstyles. Go for a minimal makeup look with a light foundation, subtle blush, and a nude lipstick shade. Keep your hair simple and sleek with a low ponytail or a messy bun.

Incorporating minimalist fashion into your wardrobe is a

great way to achieve a timeless and elegant look that can be easily dressed up or down. Embrace the simplicity of minimalist style and focus on quality over quantity, and you'll be able to create a chic and sophisticated wardrobe that will stand the test of time.

Hip Hop - How to Replicate the Baggy and Bold Style

Hip-hop fashion was a defining trend of the 90s inspired by hip-hop music and culture. Hip-hop fashion was about expressing individuality and creativity through clothing, focusing on baggy, oversized, comfortable, and functional pieces. Bold colors, striking patterns, and athletic-inspired silhouettes characterized the style.

Pair a baggy t-shirt or sweatshirt with loose-fitting jeans or joggers to replicate the hip-hop style. Look for pieces that have bold patterns or graphics, and don't be afraid to mix and match different colors and textures.

Accessories are an essential part of hip-hop fashion. Opt for a chunky gold chain or a statement watch, and wear a baseball cap or a bucket hat. Sneakers are a must-have for any hip-hop outfit, with classic styles like Nike Air Jordans, Reebok Classics, or Adidas Superstars being popular.

Makeup and hair should be bold and confident, focusing on statement hairstyles and makeup looks. Experiment with bright colors and bold patterns; don't be afraid to try new styles.

Incorporating hip-hop fashion into your wardrobe is a great way to express your individuality and creativity through clothing. Embrace the baggy and bold hip-hop fashion style, and don't be afraid to mix and match different colors, textures, and patterns. You can easily rock the hip-hop look with the right attitude and a confident sense of style.

Retro - How to Incorporate Nostalgic Fashion Trends Today

The 1990s was a decade of revival and nostalgia, with many fashion trends harkening back to earlier decades. Retro fashion was all about borrowing elements from the past and incorporating them into modern outfits. From vintage-inspired clothing to throwback accessories, retro fashion was a celebration of history and a nod to the future.

To incorporate retro fashion into your wardrobe, start with a statement piece inspired by an earlier decade. Look for vintage-inspired clothing, such as high-waisted jeans, flared trousers, or a cropped top. You can incorporate retro prints and patterns like polka dots, stripes, or floral prints.

Accessories are an essential part of retro fashion, and they can be used to add a touch of nostalgia to your outfit. Opt for vintage-inspired accessories like cat-eye sunglasses, an old-fashioned watch, or a headscarf. You can also incorporate retro-inspired jewelry like hoop earrings or a charm bracelet.

Makeup and hair can also incorporate retro fashion into your look. Go for a vintage-inspired hairstyle, such as a bob or a beehive, and experiment with bold makeup looks, such as winged eyeliner or a bold red lip.

Incorporating retro fashion into your wardrobe is a great

way to add a touch of nostalgia and personality to your style. Embrace the past and experiment with different eras, from the 50s to the 80s, to create a retro-inspired look that's uniquely yours.

Street Style - How to Replicate the Bold Looks of Streetwear

Streetwear fashion was a defining trend of the 90s inspired by the urban landscape and the music scene. Streetwear fashion was about making a statement through bold colors, patterns, and graphics. Baggy clothing, oversized silhouettes, and an emphasis on athletic-inspired pieces characterized the style.

Start with a statement t-shirt or sweatshirt with bold graphics or logos to replicate the streetwear look. Pair it with baggy or oversized pants, such as cargo pants or loose-fitting jeans. Streetwear is all about layering, so add a denim or bomber jacket to your shirt for an extra layer of style.

Accessories are an essential part of streetwear fashion. Opt for chunky sneakers or boots, and wear a baseball cap or a beanie on your head. Add some bling with a statement watch or a chain necklace.

Makeup and hair should be simple and natural, focusing on healthy skin and effortless hairstyles. Go for a natural makeup look with mascara and tinted lip balm. Keep your hair in a low ponytail or a messy bun.

Incorporating streetwear fashion into your wardrobe is a great way to add a touch of boldness and individuality to your style. Embrace the oversized silhouettes and bold graphics of streetwear fashion, and don't be afraid to experiment with different colors and textures. You can easily rock the streetwear look with the right attitude and confidence.

The Runway: How 90s Fashion Influenced High Fashion

The 1990s was a decade of creativity and innovation in the fashion industry, and many of the trends that emerged during this time had a lasting impact on high fashion. From grunge to minimalism to hip-hop, the 90s was a time of experimentation and individuality that inspired designers worldwide.

Grunge fashion was one of the most influential trends of the 90s, significantly impacting high fashion. Designers like Marc Jacobs and Anna Sui incorporated grunge elements into their collections, such as plaid shirts, combat boots, and distressed denim. Grunge-inspired fashion rejected high fashion's traditional glamour and elegance and paved the way for a new era of street-inspired style.

Minimalism was another trend that emerged during the 90s and significantly influenced high fashion. Designers like Calvin Klein and Jil Sander embraced minimalist aesthetics with clean lines, simple shapes, and neutral colors. Minimalism was a reaction to the excesses of the 80s, and it represented a return to simplicity and elegance in fashion.

Hip-hop fashion also significantly influenced high style during the 90s. Designers like Tommy Hilfiger and Ralph Lauren incorporated hip-hop elements into their collections, such as baggy pants, oversized t-shirts, and flashy jewelry. Hip-hop-inspired fashion was about expressing individuality and creativity through clothing, and it paved the way for a new era of street-inspired style.

Incorporating the influence of 90s fashion into high fashion was a game-changer that paved the way for a new era of fashion design. The 90s was a decade of experimentation and creativity that inspires designers today. Whether you're a fashion lover or a designer, understanding the influence of 90s fashion on high fashion is critical to understanding style evolution in the 21st century.

Athleisure - How to Replicate the Sporty and Comfortable Look

Athleisure fashion was a defining trend of the 90s that combined sporty and comfortable clothing with everyday fashion. Athleisure fashion was about wearing dysfunctional, comfortable dresses while still looking stylish. Athletic-inspired pieces, such as track pants, sneakers, and sweatshirts, characterized the style.

To replicate the athleisure look, start with a pair of joggers or track pants and pair it with a simple t-shirt or sweatshirt. Opt for comfortable and breathable fabrics, such as cotton or spandex blends. Look for pieces designed for performance and comfort but can also be styled for everyday wear.

Accessories are an essential part of athleisure fashion, and they can add a touch of style and personality to your outfit. Opt for a pair of sleek sneakers or slides, and add a baseball cap or a beanie to your head. A simple backpack or crossbody bag can complete the look.

Makeup and hair should be simple and natural, focusing on healthy skin and effortless hairstyles. Go for a natural makeup look with mascara and tinted lip balm. Keep your hair in a low ponytail or a messy bun.

Incorporating athleisure fashion into your wardrobe is a great way to achieve a sporty, comfortable look that can be easily dressed up or down. Embrace the functional and comfortable pieces of athleisure fashion, and add your personal touch to create a look that's uniquely yours.

Accessories - How to Accessorize 90s Trends with a Modern Twist

Accessories are an essential part of fashion, and they can add a touch of personality and style to any outfit. When it comes to accessorizing 90s fashion trends, there are plenty of ways to incorporate modern elements into the mix.

For grunge fashion, you can add a touch of modernity by incorporating statement jewelry, such as oversized earrings or a bold cuff bracelet. A pair of sleek ankle boots or a leather backpack can add a touch of modernity to the grunge look.

For minimalist fashion, keep accessories simple and understated. A delicate pendant necklace or a pair of stud earrings can add a touch of elegance to a minimalistic outfit. A sleek clutch or a modern watch can also add a touch of sophistication.

For hip-hop fashion, add a modern twist by incorporating designer sneakers or luxury streetwear pieces, such as a statement jacket or an embellished sweatshirt. A pair of statement sunglasses or a designer belt can add a touch of modernity to the hip-hop look.

You can add a modern twist to retro fashion by incorporating statement accessories, such as a bold scarf or a statement handbag. Trendy footwear, such as sleek ankle boots or stylish sneakers, can add a contemporary touch to the retro-inspired outfit.

For streetwear fashion, accessorize with statement pieces, such as a bold watch or a chunky chain necklace. Modern footwear, such as designer sneakers or ankle boots, can also add a touch of sophistication to the street-inspired outfit.

Incorporating modern accessories into 90s fashion trends is a great way to add a contemporary touch to your style. Embrace the individuality and creativity of fashion, and don't be afraid to mix and match different eras and techniques to create a look that's uniquely yours.

Beauty - How 90s Beauty Trends Are Making a Comeback

The 90s was a decade of bold and adventurous beauty trends returning in the 21st century. From grunge-inspired makeup to minimalist beauty routines, the 90s was a decade of experimentation and individuality that inspires beauty trends today.

Grunge-inspired makeup was a defining trend of the 90s that's coming back in the 21st century. Dark, smoky eyes and bold, matte lips were the hallmarks of grunge makeup, and they continue to be popular today. Blend a dark eyeshadow along your upper and lower lash lines to achieve the grunge look. Pair it with bold, matte lipstick in a deep shade, such as burgundy or brown.

Minimalism was another trend that emerged during the 90s and continues to inspire beauty trends today. Minimalist beauty routines use a few high-quality products that enhance natural beauty. Embrace the minimalist trend by investing in a quality skincare routine emphasizing hydration and protection. Opt for a simple makeup look with mascara and tinted lip balm.

Another trend that's making a comeback from the 90s is hair accessories. From scrunchies to hair clips, hair accessories are a fun and playful way to add a touch of personality to your look. Opt for a simple hairstyle, such as a low ponytail or a messy bun, and add a bold hair accessory, such as a statement clip or a colorful scrunchie.

Incorporating 90s beauty trends into your routine is a great way to add a touch of individuality and creativity to your look. Embrace the bold and adventurous beauty trends of the 90s, and don't be afraid to experiment with different styles and techniques to create a look that's uniquely yours.

Denim: How to Replicate the Ultimate 90s Staple

Denim was a defining trend of the 90s that continues to be a staple in fashion today. From high-waisted jeans to denim jackets, denim was the ultimate casual and versatile fabric that could be dressed up or down for any occasion.

To replicate the ultimate 90s denim look, start with a pair of high-waisted jeans or denim shorts. Pair it with a simple t-shirt or crop top for a classic look, or dress it up with a blouse or blazer for a more formal occasion. Denim on denim was also a popular trend in the 90s, so don't be afraid to experiment with different washes and styles of denim.

Accessories are an essential part of the denim look, and they can be used to add a touch of personality and style to any outfit. Opt for a pair of sleek sneakers or boots, and add a statement belt or necklace for a touch of glam. A denim jacket or vest can also add style to any outfit.

Makeup and hair should be kept simple and natural to complement denim's casual and versatile nature. Go for a natural makeup look with mascara and tinted lip balm. Keep your hair in a low ponytail or a messy bun for a laid-back look.

Incorporating denim into your wardrobe is a great way to achieve a classic, versatile look that never goes out of style. Embrace the different types and washes of denim, and experiment with different ways to dress it up or down for any occasion. With the right attitude and a confident sense of style, you can easily rock the ultimate 90s denim look.

Grunge Glam: How to Add a Touch of Grunge to Your Nighttime Look

Grunge fashion was all about rejecting the traditional glamour of high fashion and embracing a more casual and rugged aesthetic. However, grunge can also be incorporated into a nighttime look for a touch of edge and rebelliousness.

Start with a black or dark-colored dress or skirt to achieve the grunge glam look. Opt for a flowy or oversized silhouette reminiscent of the grunge era. Pair it with chunky boots or heels for a touch of edginess.

Accessories are an essential part of the grunge glam look, and they can be used to add a touch of personality and style to any outfit. Opt for a statement necklace or a bold cuff bracelet for a touch of glam, or go for a leather choker or studded belt for a touch of edginess.

Makeup is a crucial element of the grunge glam look. Go for a bold, smoky eye with dark eyeshadow and black eyeliner. Pair it with bold, matte lipstick in a deep shade, such as burgundy or brown. Keep the rest of your makeup minimal and natural to balance the dramatic eye and lip.

Hair should be kept messy and textured for a grunge glam look. Embrace your natural texture, or add some volume and texture with a texturizing or sea salt spray. A messy updo or tousled waves can add a touch of effortless glamour to the grunge look.

Incorporating grunge into your nighttime look is a great way to add a touch of edge and rebelliousness to your style. Embrace the casual and rugged aesthetic of grunge fashion, and add a touch of glam with bold makeup and statement accessories. You can easily rock the grunge glam look with the right attitude and a confident sense of style.

Iconic Looks: How to Replicate the Most Memorable 90s Fashion Moments

The 90s was a decade of memorable fashion moments that continue to inspire fashion trends today. From red carpet looks to street style, the 90s was a time of experimentation and individuality that produced some of the most iconic fashion moments ever.

One of the most memorable fashion moments of the 90s was the slip-dress trend. Made famous by fashion icons like Kate Moss and Courtney Love, the slip dress was all about understated sexiness and elegance. To replicate the slip dress look, opt for a simple silk slip dress in a neutral color, such as black or white. Pair it with delicate jewelry and strappy sandals for a touch of sophistication.

Another iconic 90s fashion moment was the grunge trend. With its ripped jeans, plaid shirts, and combat boots, grunge was all about rejecting traditional glamour and embracing a more casual and rugged aesthetic. Opt for a plaid shirt or dress, distressed denim, and chunky boots to replicate the grunge look. Accessorize with studded belts and chokers for a touch of edginess.

Hip-hop fashion was another defining trend of the 90s, and it was all about expressing individuality and creativity through clothing. Oversized t-shirts, baggy pants, and flashy jewelry were the hallmarks of hip-hop fashion. Opt for baggy pants, an oversized sweatshirt, and chunky sneakers to replicate the hip-hop look. Accessorize with statement jewelry, such as chunky gold chains and hoop earrings.

Incorporating iconic 90s fashion moments into your wardrobe is a great way to pay homage to the decade of creativity and individuality. Embrace the different styles and trends of the 90s, and add your personal touch to create a look that's uniquely yours. With the right attitude and a confident sense of style, you can easily replicate the most memorable 90s fashion moments.

Fashion Forward: How to Take 90s Inspiration to the Next Level

While the 90s was a decade of iconic fashion trends, incorporating these trends into your style doesn't mean you have to look like you stepped out of a time capsule. With simple updates and modern twists, you can take 90s inspiration to the next level and create a fashion-forward and contemporary look.

One way to update 90s fashion trends is to mix and match different styles and eras. For example, you can pair a grunge-inspired plaid shirt with a sleek leather skirt, a statement necklace, or bold heels. Don't be afraid to experiment with different textures, colors, and patterns to create a unique and unexpected look.

Another way to take 90s inspiration to the next level is to incorporate modern silhouettes and fabrics into your outfits. For example, pair a minimalist slip dress with a trendy bomber jacket or stylish sneakers. Look for pieces incorporating current fashion trends, such as oversized sleeves or asymmetrical hemlines, to add a touch of modernity to your look.

Accessories are another essential element of fashion-forward 90s style. Incorporate modern accessories, such as statement jewelry or a sleek clutch, into your outfit to add a touch of sophistication and glamour. A stylish watch or a designer belt can also add a contemporary touch to your look.

Makeup and hair are crucial elements of fashion-forward 90s style. Embrace the natural and effortless look of the 90s, but add a touch of modernity with a bold lipstick or a statement eye. Keep your hair simple and sleek with a low ponytail or tousled waves.

Incorporating 90s inspiration into your style is a great way to pay homage to the decade of individuality and creativity. However, taking 90s inspiration to the next level requires incorporating modern elements and updating classic looks with new twists. Experiment with different styles and trends to create a look that's uniquely yours and fashion-forward.

Conclusion: How 90s Fashion Trends Continue to Inspire Modern Style

The 90s was a decade of iconic fashion trends that inspire modern style today. From grunge-inspired looks to minimalist beauty routines, the 90s was a time of creativity and individuality that produced some of the most memorable fashion moments ever.

While 90s fashion may seem like a thing of the past, it inspires modern style in countless ways. The possibilities are endless, from incorporating vintage denim into a contemporary look to updating grunge-inspired outfits with modern twists.

One of the reasons why 90s fashion continues to inspire modern style is because of its focus on individuality and creativity. The 90s was a time of rejecting traditional glamour and embracing a more casual and rugged aesthetic. This focus on personal expression and identity resonates with modern fashion trends prioritizing inclusivity and self-expression.

Whether you're a fan of the minimalist beauty routines or the bold and edgy grunge-inspired looks, there's something for everyone in 90s fashion. Incorporate these trends into your wardrobe and embrace your style to create a look that's uniquely yours.

In conclusion, 90s fashion trends inspire modern style in

countless ways. These trends, from vintage denim to grunge glam, are a testament to fashion's enduring creativity and individuality. Embrace these trends and add your personal touch to create a look that's fashion-forward and uniquely yours.

Afterword

Looking back on the fashion trends of the 90s, it's clear that this decade significantly impacted the fashion world. From grunge-inspired looks to minimalist beauty routines, the 90s was a time of creativity, individuality, and self-expression that inspires fashion trends today.

One of the reasons why 90s fashion was so significant is because it represented a rejection of traditional glamour and a focus on personal expression. For example, the grunge trend was about rejecting conventional beauty standards and embracing a more casual and rugged aesthetic. This focus on individual expression and individuality inspires modern fashion trends that prioritize inclusivity and self-expression.

Another reason why 90s fashion was so significant is that it represented a fusion of different styles and cultures. Hip-hop fashion, for example, was influenced by the music and style of urban communities, while the punk and alternative rock scenes influenced grunge fashion. This fusion of styles and cultures inspires modern fashion trends celebrating diversity and inclusivity.

As we continue to navigate the fashion world, it's important to remember the significance of 90s fashion trends and their impact on the industry. By embracing the creativity and individuality of the 90s, we can create a fashion landscape that celebrates diversity, inclusivity, and self-expression.